The HOLIDAY WREATH BOOK

80 Wreaths to Celebrate
Birthdays, Anniversaries
& Holidays
Throughout the Year

ERIC CARLSON

A Sterling/Lark Book
Sterling Publishing Co., Inc.   New York

Photography: Evan Bracken
Art Director: Chris Colando
Cover Design: Karen Nelson
Production: Chris Colando and Elaine Thompson

Library of Congress Cataloging-in-Publication Data
Carlson, Eric, 1952-
      The holiday wreath book : 80 wreaths to celebrate birthdays,
anniversaries & holidays throughout the year / by Eric Carlson
           p.   cm.
      "Sterling/Lark books."
      Includes bibliographical references and index.
      ISBN 0-8069-8696-4
      1. Wreaths. 2. Holiday decorations. I. Title.
SB449.5.W74C39 1992
745.92'6—dc20   91-47698
                                                    CIP

10 9 8 7 6 5 4 3 2 1

A Sterling/Lark Book

Produced by Altamont Press
    50 College Street Asheville, NC 28801, USA

Published in 1992 by Sterling Publishing Co., Inc.
    387 Park Avenue South, New York, NY 10016

© 1992, Altamont Press

Distributed in Canada by Sterling Publishing,
    c/o Canadian Manda Group,
    P.O. Box 920, Station U, Toronto, Ontario M8Z 5P9
Distributed in the United Kingdom by Cassell PLC, Villiers House,
    41/47 Strand, London WC2N 5JE, England
Distributed in Australia by Capricorn Link Ltd.,
    P.O. Box 665 Lane Cove, NSW 2066

ISBN 0-8069-8696-4

The HOLIDAY WREATH BOOK

CONTENTS

W **H** **A** **T** is a wreath? If you haven't discovered the joys of making your own wreaths, you will probably think of Christmas...of greenery circles...of pine needles...and holly berries...of bows and red ribbon...all dusted with snowflakes and hung over a brass door knocker; images that evoke memories of warm and happy times with family and friends sharing the traditions that bind us together across generations; traditions that can be and should be and will be preserved by making still more circular, pine, holly, red-ribbon, front-door Christmas wreaths.

But what else is a wreath? Could it be an oval? Or a square? Or a heart shape? Can it be made of wood? Or metal? Or plastic? Might you display your wreath on a table or hang it from the ceiling? Could you make one to celebrate Easter? Or Halloween? Or New Year's Eve? How about a birthday or graduation wreath? Why not make a wreath to remind the family of a coming vacation or retirement? After all, if wreaths can rekindle memories of Christmas past, might they not do likewise for other holidays and occasions, sparking similar joyful reminiscences each time we glance at them or exhume them from storage for a perennial observance?

To all of the above, the answer is a resounding YES! You can create any sort of wreath out of anything imaginable for any occasion you choose. That's what this book is all about. Wreaths are an invitation to share in an experience or emotion. They are totems lovingly wrought with familiar imagery to remind us of our universal kinship.

The traditional and most common shape for the wreath—the circle—has been revered as a symbol of natural harmony throughout human history. Early tribal cultures perceived of the world as a great circle formed by the horizon surrounding them, a shape they found repeated in countless forms: the sun, the moon, the eyes, the ripples from a stone tossed in the water. Perhaps while drawing a circle in the sand, watching the end come around to join the beginning, our ancestors first began to wonder about the mysterious cycles of day and night, of summer and winter, of planting and harvest, of birth and death.

The circle was found to be practical as well as mystical. Campfires, tents, huts, baskets, and pottery were more efficient when made circular. Later castle parapets, walled cities, church domes, arches, and the wheel provided further evidence of the circle's power.

So it is hardly surprising that religions worldwide revere the circle as a sacred image. The Chinese symbol for yin and yang, the Hindu wheel of life and death, the luminous halo over the saints in Christian art all take the form of a circle. Lowered onto the head of a ruler, the circular halo became a crown, the principal symbol of royalty.

It is from this latter application that wreaths may have originated. In ancient Greece and Rome, great warriors, athletes, poets, and orators were rewarded for their accomplishments with crowns of laurel (hence the term "earning your laurels"). It's unlikely that such hard-won symbols of honor would be hastily discarded, so it seems reasonable to speculate that these hoops of vine and foliage might have been hung on the wall, to serve both as decoration and as a treasured reminder of previous achievement.

Through the centuries and around the world, circlets of flowers have been tradi-tional adornments at spring festivals. Harvest celebrants commonly display stalks of grain woven into circles, which serve not only to commemorate the occasion, but also as a practical method of drying seeds for the coming year's planting. More than mere decoration, these wreaths acknowledge the interconnection of one season or event with the cycles of life and nature.

Which is why we make wreaths today. The evergreens on a Christmas wreath bring the forest fragrance indoors and remind us that beyond the cold harsh winter there will be rebirth in the spring. The ribbons and candy exalt the spirit of giving and recall the joys of childhood Christmas.

Likewise the fruits on a harvest wreath celebrate the season's bounty while the golden leaves remind us of perpetual change.

On Easter, a floral shrouded cross can honor the season's deep religious significance or a cuddly bunny can recall the innocent laughter of children scurrying for hidden eggs. As in Victorian times, the intricate symbolism of flowers can compose lasting personal messages of affection and devotion in wedding, anniversary, and Valentine's wreaths.

These symbols have withstood the tests of time and continue to offer endless possibilities for exciting new wreaths, as most of the designs in this book will show. But wreath makers today are using new and unusual materials in imaginative ways to commemorate all sorts of holidays and occasions. Like more traditional wreaths, the choice of materials remains rooted in symbolism but—as you will see from their creations—the accent is on fun.

Which is why we invite you to join the thousands who have discovered that wreath making is a rewarding personal expression of thoughtfulness and holiday spirit. The basic techniques of wreath making—fully outlined in the opening section—are quite simple and easy to master. Once you've learned to use floral picks, wire, and a glue gun, making a wreath is largely a matter of selecting and arranging your materials.

So browse through the pages, collect some ideas, and make a wreath. There's no need to wait until Christmas anymore...

M A K I N G your own wreath begins with your choice of a base or form. Since each type base comes with inherent restrictions and possibilities, your selection will depend largely on how you wish the finished wreath to look.

Your first consideration will be the shape. Next you must decide whether or not the base will be completely covered or exposed as a visual feature of the completed wreath. Lastly you'll need to choose a base material that is appropriate for the elements you plan to attach.

Except in those cases where the shape of your wreath will be the focus of the design (as in a heart-shaped wreath for Valentine's day) you'll probably choose a circular or oval shaped base. Since this is the basic, time honored shape for most wreaths, the circle will offer you the widest range of commercially available bases, although hearts and ovals are also easy to find.

But don't feel confined by tradition. Sheets of styrofoam can be cut and wire can be bent into any shape that suits your fancy. Or you can decorate other objects that might suggest wreath ideas, like a picture frame, a clock face, a mirror, or even an automobile hubcap.

Unless you've chosen your base for its visual appeal or significance to the occasion, you will probably cover it, either with a wrapping such as ribbon or with natural or artificial plant materials. So in most cases, the premade bases found in any craft store should suit your needs. Vine, straw, wire, and foam are the most commonly available. Just remember that if you need an unusual shape, these and other materials can be used to make your own bases at home.

V I N E S Probably the oldest type of wreath base, vines remain one of the most versatile and popular wreath components. These bases are strong enough to support heavy items. The vines offer limitless surfaces for attachment with either hot glue or wire. As an added enticement, vine bases are often attractive enough to be left unadorned, either in their natural color or coated with spray paint or glitter.

While vine bases are readily available just about anywhere, it's also quite easy to make your own. Grape, honeysuckle, and wisteria are the most commonly used, but almost any type of vine or root will do. Just take several different lengths of vine about 2 to 5 feet (61 to 152 cm) long and form a hoop the size of the desired wreath. Wrap the longer vine ends around and around the others, adding more vines until you have the proper thickness.

S T R A W Another popular base that's easy to find in stores, these are frequently covered with moss as a floral background. They can be wrapped with ribbon to create a smoother colorful surface, or you can hot glue materials directly to the straw. You can also attach items by wiring through the straw or by sticking floral picks into the base. Round straw bases can be reshaped to create an oval, and heart shapes are also available.

You can make your own straw base in any shape you like out of hay, alfalfa, or other kinds of dried grass. Start with a handful about 1 foot (30 cm) long and 1-1/2" (4 cm) thick with one end slightly thinner than the other. Begin

wrapping around the straw with heavy floral wire, adding straw at the thinner end and repeating until the length reaches the desired circumference. Overlap the ends and continue wrapping wire around the base several times.

F O A M These inexpensive, plain white bases don't look like much when unadorned, but they offer a wide variety of possibilities for the imaginative wreath maker. When wrapped with colored ribbon, the smooth surface makes for a sleek satiny look. Or you can cover the foam with moss or grated cinnamon. Even if you plan to hide the surface completely with attached items, it is usually advisable to wrap the base first, since hot glue can melt the foam. For fresh flower wreaths, you can also find bases made of floral foam.

If you plan to make an unusually shaped wreath, you can cut a base out of styrofoam and cover it with moss, bark, ribbon, fabric, or other material. Or use foam core mounting board for a thin flat base that can be spray painted any color you choose.

W I R E Whether purchased or shaped by hand, wire bases are ideal for creating moss or greenery backgrounds for your wreaths. Double-wire ring

forms can be packed with sweet Annie, artemisia, or any sort of moss and wrapped with wire or thread. Moss can also be rolled up in a sheet of chicken wire and wired together at the ends to create a base. Boughs of white pine, holly, hemlock, arbor vitae, red cedar, or similar greenery can be wired onto a hoop of heavy gauge wire (some designers use coat hangers) to make an evergreen wreath. A painted coil of barbed wire makes a surprisingly attractive—though quite prickly—wreath base.

P U R C H A S E D W R E A T H S If you need a base covered in evergreens or some other traditional material but don't feel like making your own, you can simply buy a pre-made wreath and dress it up. Unadorned natural and artificial wreaths are available at craft stores, especially at Christmas time. These can be the basis for wonderfully personal wreath designs without the added step of covering a base. On many fake evergreen wreaths the wire branches can be bent around ribbons and other objects, avoiding the need for hot glue and allowing you to disassemble the wreath for a new design next year.

F O U N D For special occasion and novelty wreaths, almost anything you can hang on the wall (and many things you can't) could be used as a wreath base: the colored plastic hoops from a child's ring-toss game, a ship's wheel, the wire frame from an old lampshade, a pie plate, an inner tube, even a toilet seat. Don't hesitate to improvise.

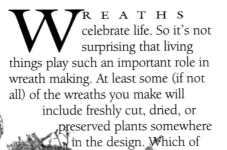

WREATHS celebrate life. So it's not surprising that living things play such an important role in wreath making. At least some (if not all) of the wreaths you make will include freshly cut, dried, or preserved plants somewhere in the design. Which of these you choose will depend largely on how long you wish your wreath to remain attractive.

Some of the most glorious wreaths imaginable can be created using fresh flowers—perfect for a gift or one-day celebration—but their beauty will quickly fade. Evergreens maintain their cheery bright color throughout the Christmas season, filling the air with a crisp woodsy scent, but they will grow brittle and crumble if stored. Dried flowers and grasses offer a more subdued palette than their fresh counterparts, but these wreaths can be displayed year-round and even stored if necessary. Using herbs in your wreaths adds yet another dimension. Not only do these offer bright colors and a pleasing fragrance when freshly cut, but many herbs will change tone and texture attractively as they dry.

FRESH FLOWERS Wreath makers who enjoy gardening should consider adding fresh flowers to their creations. To do so you will need a few special accesories. Wet foam or moss bases, available at florist shops, will allow you to prolong the life of a fresh flower wreath with occasional applications of water. Or you can make a wet floral base out of sphagnum moss rolled in chicken wire. If you need only a few fresh flowers, a wet-foam block can be wired to the wreath base. Also available through florists are small plastic tubes that can be wired or hot glued into a wreath to hold enough water to sustain a fresh flower for several days. This system also allows you to exchange old flowers for fresh ones as they wilt.

DRIED FLOWERS Though not quite as vibrant in color or fragrance as flowers freshly picked from the garden, the long lasting beauty of dried flowers makes them the preferred choice of most floral wreath makers.

Drying your own flowers is easy. Almost any garden or wildflower is worth a try. Pick the flowers just before they've completely opened—preferably on a warm day—after any dew or raindrops have evaporated.

Simply tie the flowers in bunches by the stems and hang them upside down in a dark, well ventilated area for four to fourteen days. Or you can cut the drying time in half by placing flowers in a container with a moisture-absorbing chemical such as silica gel. You'll want to experiment, since different plants work better with different techniques.

Dried flowers are somewhat fragile (especially those dried with chemicals) so the less they are handled, the longer they will last. Also remember to keep dried flower wreaths away from direct sunlight, which tends to fade their colors.

EVERGREENS A staple component of Christmas wreaths, evergreens have been used in holiday celebrations since the days of ancient Rome. Sturdy enough to last through the holiday season,

many types of evergreens have the added enticement of emitting those wonderful forest fragrances we love to bring into our homes at Christmas time. Varieties of pine, holly, hemlock, cedar, boxwood, and ivy are popular choices for wreath making. Evergreen boughs can be wired to a straw or wire base as a background or hot glued on in smaller pieces as an accessory.

CONES, NUTS, SEEDS, AND PODS Long lasting and easy to find, these fruits of nature can add texture, color, and visual interest to wreaths of all sorts. Pine cones are a traditional (and obvious) element to use with evergreens. Milkweed and okra pods are popular in harvest wreaths. Large seed clusters and dried wildflower seed heads are frequently used with dried flowers and other naturals.

IT USED to be that artificial plants looked exactly as their name implies: obviously fake. But as you will see from many of the wreaths in this book, even the focused eye of a close-up camera often can't distinguish genuine flowers, fruits, and greenery from their artificial counterparts.

While many wreath makers prefer to use natural materials exclusively, modern artificials offer significant advantages for certain types of wreaths. A fresh flower wreath is a rare and beautiful feast of color and fragrance (and well worth the effort to create), but if you want to display a floral wreath for any length of time, you'll need to use artificials. A fresh pine wreath will last a season outside or it can fill your home with delightful forest scents (reason enough to make one), but only artificials will allow you to create a holiday keepsake that can be displayed for many years to come.

Fake flowers are especially easy to use, as their wire stems can be readily bent around or poked into the wreath base. Plastic berries and other fruits are likewise easy to attach. On wreaths made of artificial greenery the branches can be bent around ribbons or other objects to secure them. Many first-time wreath makers begin by dressing up a pre-made artificial greenery wreath. Several of the Christmas wreaths pictured in this book were made this way, although you may not recognize them by looking. Another convenient feature of artificial materials is that they are reusable. You can disassemble a wreath you've grown tired of and use the components in new designs.

The already extensive variety of readily available artificials increases every year. You should have no trouble finding materials to achieve any look you have in mind. Recently manufacturers have

begun to sell a wide range of preserved plant materials dyed with colors never intended by nature. These offer much of the durability of artificials, the textures and forms of natural plants, and striking new visual effects for your

wreaths. The dramatic Christmas wreath on page 39 could not have been made without these new dyed naturals. (Unless you know where to find a burgundy holly tree!)

In the end the choice of whether to go natural or artificial will be up to you. Just as some prefer the convenience of an artificial Christmas tree, others would never think of having one in their home. Both have their advantages and disadvantages. Just don't limit yourself. The world of wreath making is as vast as you allow it to be.

MANY beautiful wreaths are designed with no distinct focal point, relying instead on a seamless mixture of similar or contrasting colors, shapes, and textures to achieve an eye-pleasing whole. This is especially true of floral and herbal wreaths in which only one or two plant species may be used. While there might be striking dramatic elements in the composition, no single item dominates.

Another approach is to anchor the design with a central component or arrangement and fill in around it. These focal points may be chosen purely for visual appeal or because of their symbolic significance. Groupings of fruit, nuts, or seed pods—suggesting a bountiful harvest—are often used to highlight autumn wreaths. For an Easter wreath you might include a cross to commemorate the holiday's religious significance or use a cuddly bunny and colored eggs to celebrate a child's view of the season.

By far the most popular embellishment—especially for Christmas wreaths—is a brightly colored ribbon tied in a bow. Ribbons can also be used to wrap a wreath base, to make flowers and other decorations, to entwine through vines or greenery, or just to dangle here and there as dashes of color and movement. Every year manufacturers introduce exciting new ribbon styles, patterns, colors, and materials. Here are just a few of the more popular ones.

S A T I N Available in a wide variety of colors and thicknesses, satin ribbon is a good choice for covering a foam wreath base. It may not be the best choice for beginners however because it cannot be re-used if a mistake is made in tying.

C O T T O N Perfect for the homespun "country" look, cotton is a good ribbon for beginners, since any creases can be smoothed with a hot iron. Wide sizes can be cut into thinner strips if necessary.

P A P E R Extremely versatile and simple to work with, paper ribbon ties easily into a variety of bows. It adds an interesting texture to your wreath, holds its shape well after tying, and can be re-shaped if crushed. Paper ribbon can be re-used again and again, making it an ideal choice for beginners. It also holds up well on outdoor wreaths.

V E L V E T A bit more demanding for the beginner because it is easily crushed and not re-usable, velvet ribbons give a very formal, traditional look to a wreath.

C E L L O P H A N E Easy to use and re-use, the shiny metallic colors of cellophane ribbon add flash and sparkle to your special occasion wreaths. Unlike many ribbons, cellophane will not fade in sunlight.

F R E N C H Lined with thin strips of wire, French ribbons will hold any shape you give them. A crushed bow can be easily bent back into shape, making this an ideal choice for wreaths that will be stored or shipped.

L A C E A favorite for wedding and anniversary wreaths, lace ribbon has a soft romantic look. It needs to be very stiff when purchased to hold its shape. Unstiffened lace can be placed on top of a satin or cotton ribbon and tied with it.

R A F F I A The natural look and texture of raffia make it an obvious choice for wreaths made of flowers, herbs, and other plant materials.

N o w that you've chosen a base for your wreath and assembled your decorative materials, all that remains is to put them together. This may seem intimidating at first, but once you've spent just a short time acquainting yourself with a glue gun, floral picks, and wire you'll be able to make just about any wreath you've ever seen or imagined.

In most cases the best way of attaching an item to the base will be fairly obvious, and if an alternative method seems suitable, it probably is. Your decision will depend largely on the weight and texture of the item, the type of base, and how best to conceal the attachment.

FLORAL PICKS
These are to the wreath maker what nails are to the carpenter. Nothing more than small sharpened sticks with thin wires attached at the blunt ends, floral picks are indispensable for securing natural materials to a wreath base. They can also be glued on or poked into countless other small decorative items and hot glued to the base. Floral picks are inexpensive and available in numerous colors to blend with your base or decorative elements.

To "pick" an item such as a single spray or a cluster of several small flowers, lay the stem(s) alongside the blunt end of the pick leaving enough of the sharp end exposed to insert into the base. Wrap the wire several times around the two and continue spiraling down until you have wrapped the end around the bare pick. Larger components such as pine cones and small novelty items may require a dab of hot glue to secure them to the picks.

When covering straw, foam, moss, and some vine bases, simply stick the picks into the surface at an angle and continue picking materials in at the same angle around the wreath, making sure to overlap and hide the picks as you go. On wire bases or loosely meshed vine bases, you will probably need hot glue or wire to attach your picks.

GLUE GUNS If you want to make wreaths, you really ought to have a glue gun. This safe, inexpensive, and easy-to-use tool has revolutionized the craft industry by making previously impossible attachments as quick and easy as a squeeze of the finger. The hot glue goes where you want it, dries quickly, holds amazingly well, and can be peeled off most surfaces if you make a mistake.

Since glue guns use heat to melt the glue, a few precautions are in order. Keep your gun on its stand (or on a plate) and out of children's reach when hot and not in use. Arrange the power cord so it won't get snagged and unplug it when you're finished. If you are using a foam base, test the surface with a dab of hot glue to make sure it won't melt. If it does, wrap the base first with ribbon, moss, fabric or other material.

When attaching things with a glue gun you may find yourself dragging fine strands of glue across your work. Don't worry, as these are easily removed later. When gluing a large item, hold it in place for at least a minute to ensure a good bond. Very heavy decorations may need to be wired on first and reinforced with hot glue.

A glue gun can also be used to make plastic letters, numbers, and other shapes to dress up your holiday wreaths. Simply apply a thin film of non-stick cooking spray to a piece of glass and draw anything you like on it with hot glue. The shape will peel off easily, remaining firm but flexible. You can sprinkle glitter into the glue while it's hot or spray-paint the shapes when cool. Then glue or pick them into your wreath.

WIRE Heavy decorations, novelties, large bows, bunches of greenery, and other cumbersome objects are best secured to a wreath base with wire. While any suitably strong wire will do, most wreath makers use floral wire due to its low cost, flexibility, and availability in numerous thicknesses (or gauges). The challenge is to find a way to attach the item without leaving the wire exposed, a problem often solved with a final addition of tastefully concealing flowers, greenery, or ribbon. Wiring can be used on any base, but vine bases are especially well suited, as they offer numerous points of attachment without the need for wrapping wire completely around the base.

APPLICATION ORDER It's generally best to secure the largest objects to your wreath first, since these may require wiring or other attachment techniques that can later be concealed by smaller elements. Save your most fragile items for last to avoid damaging them when adding other materials.

A popular method of making floral wreaths is to begin by covering the inner and outer edges of the base with a single flower or grass, picking overlapping clusters in one direction and turning the base as you work. When you get around to the first cluster, lift it up and secure the last cluster beneath it. Use the same process and a variety of different materials to cover the front face of the wreath. Then add a few special accent clusters last.

W H E N we think
of wreaths, we think
of Christmas. No fully
decorated holiday home would be
complete without a well-trimmed
tree, a few strings of colored lights,
some red felt mantelpiece stock-
ings, and a festive holiday wreath
for the front door. While most
wreath makers continue to include
traditional colors and materials, the
variety of Yuletide designs seems
endless. No matter how many
times you create a special wreath
for an upcoming holiday season,
you can always find exciting new
ways to make your wreaths say,
"Merry Christmas!"

PINES, red bows, and berries are probably the most common components of Christmas wreath making. Still an amazing diversity of unique designs can be created from this familiar trio. The maker of this wreath began with a store-bought base of baby's breath. She wired on the plaid ribbon bow first, then hot glued in pieces of preserved noble tip pine. Finally clusters of berries were attached to wooden picks and hot glued into place.

TRADITIONAL Christmas colors highlight this small, easy-to-make wreath that could be used as a wall or door decoration or set around a candle as a table centerpiece. Start with a purchased base of artificial greenery and hot glue first a layer of German statice, then a circle of pepperberries around the surface.

HERE'S an attractive wreath that is sure to attract roving Christmas carolers to your door. The designer used a gilded violin, singing cherubs, and stave-printed ribbon to weave a musical theme through this colorful composition of natural and artificial flora. She first wrapped a wire form with green garland and wired the violin into place. Cloth ribbon was laid over crepe paper, tied into a bow and wired to the base. A magnolia blossom with gold-painted leaves, yarrow, sumac flowers, and baby's breath (also sprayed gold) were attached with hot glue, as were the golden angels.

T I N Y twinkling Christmas lights and lacy bags of potpourri make this wreath a treat for the senses, especially in a darkened room. It was made by wrapping a wire base with greenery into which a short string of lights was woven, leaving the electrical socket hidden in back. Pink net bags of potpourri tied up with ribbon were hot glued in along with clusters of hydrangea. A bow of pink satin ribbon completes the design.

PINE boughs and holly aren't the only way to create the deep green background so popular and attractive in natural Christmas decorations. This lush wreath uses preserved oak leaves (available through craft or floral dealers) to achieve the same effect with a softer texture and a more bushy fullness. The leaves were hot glued generously around a handmade grapevine base. The bow and cane coils (another natural, craft-store item) were attached in the same manner.

F R E S H evergreen wreaths can be a delight for the nose as well as the eye, filling your home with the cheery scent of a pine forest. This fragrant Christmas wreath was made by first hot gluing sprays of blueberry cedar around a grapevine base. Then blue salvia was picked and glued into the cedar background. Finally reindeer moss was glued in at various points around the wreath.

PA L E mauve and slate blue are not the first colors that spring to mind when we think of Christmas, but the tasteful use of these hues makes this elegant Yuletide wreath an ideal decoration for rooms where bold statements in red and green might seem out of place. It was made on a purchased silk Canadian pine wreath by first weaving blue velvet ribbon and a pearl bead garland through the boughs, securing with hot glue where necessary. Next mauve silk peony blooms, iridescent clear glass balls, and pine cones were hot glued in. The pine cone bell is a purchased ornament, but you can make your own by hot gluing rows of pine cone "petals" in overlapping layers around a styrofoam bell shape.

THE imaginative use of artificial fruits, leaves, and flowers makes the central arrangement of this wreath seem to grow into its base. While the greens and reds are right at home with traditional Christmas decor, this wreath could also be displayed throughout the year or put away for other special occasions. To make it, start with a length of French ribbon looped and gathered and wired around a grapevine base. Pick and hot glue the artificial pomegranates into place and likewise attach the yellow silk magnolias. Next hot glue bunches of canella berries here and there throughout the arrangement. A small grouping of silk hens-and-chicks, canella berries, and moss is hot glued to the lower portion of the base to balance the composition.

DRIED flowers and gold ribbon give this wreath a classic Victorian look that's perfect for the Christmas holidays, yet also suitable for year-round display. It was made by first hot gluing a bow and ribbon to a purchased grapevine base. Then raffia, dried roses, carnations, German statice, and Spanish moss were likewise glued into place.

MIRRORED ornaments, a tubular ribbon bow, and a velvet-covered base combine in a design that is non-traditional, yet still evocative of the Christmas spirit. Start by wrapping a 10" (25 cm) straw wreath base with about three yards (270 cm) of wide velvet ribbon using hot glue to secure the ends. You'll need about three yards (270 cm) of tube ribbon for the bow, which is wired to the base. Berries are picked in a crescent shape across the top before German statice, cones, and gold leaves are hot glued into place. Straight pins and ribbon secure the dangling ornaments.

THE natural tendency when making a wreath is to cover the entire surface of the base with decorative materials. But sometimes it's nice to add an attractive arrangement to one area, leaving the remainder unadorned as in this asymmetrical Christmas wreath. It was made on an artificial green-ery base by first wiring on a bow of tapestry ribbon with additional streamers of ribbon cut and wired into the branches. Individual florets of silk hydrangea were picked and hot glued in along with several dried lilies. Finally silk copperberries, dried caspia, and a few gold twigs were hot glued in.

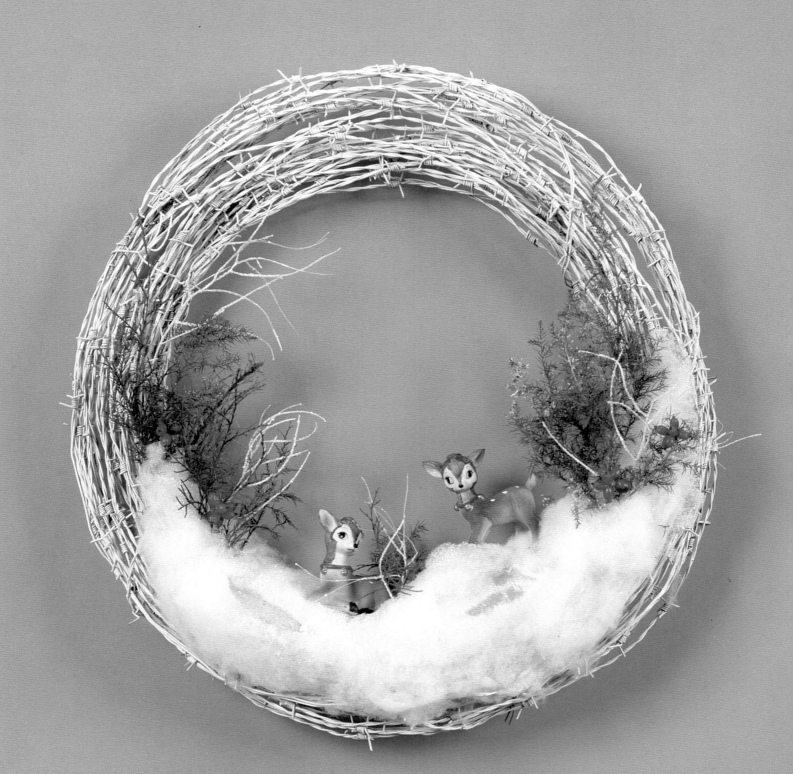

IDEAS for design elements can come from the most unlikely places. The maker of this prickly Christmas wreath was inspired by a snow-dusted roll of barbed wire she spotted hanging on a fencepost. After finding the necessary material at a local hardware store, she carefully formed a base and spray painted the wire white. To this she hot glued two ceramic deer, some puffy polyfill "snow," and mirrors to suggest a frozen pond. Sprays of cedar, painted hemlock twigs, and some dogwood berries were secured with more hot glue before adding a dusting of spray-on snow.

A SMALL Christmas tree embellished with natural materials provides the focal point for this tasteful Yule composition. The tree was removed from its base and the greenery filled out with hot-glued branches of German statice and baby's breath. Colorful organic ornaments of celosia, pepperberry, globe amaranth, and rosebuds were likewise secured to the branches. The tree was hot glued to a grapevine wreath base with a velvety red bow added to complete the design.

31

NAT U R A L and artificial materials selected in colors that complement the lovely parchment Christmas angel make this ambitious Yuletide creation a feast for the eyes. The ornament was first wired onto a large oval grapevine base. A sheaf of wheat was bound with wire and sprayed with copper paint before wiring it to the base with a bit of hot glue for reinforcement. French ribbon was worked into the grapevine and a touch of Christmas greenery added with hot glue. Next eucalyptus, lotus pods, and parchment roses were glued on. Then canella berries and gold twigs were picked in. Blue beading and moss clumps were added as final highlights.

P I N E S, poinsettias, and presents highlight this traditional, easy-to-make Christmas wreath. The designer began with a plain silk Canadian pine wreath, but you could also use a fresh or homemade base. Tiny packages, ornaments, candy canes, and silk poinsettias were hot glued in place before weaving thin white ribbon and red punch ribbon (available at florist or craft shops) into the boughs. One advantage of the artificial base is that the wire branches can be bent to hold the ribbon, saving hot glue and allowing you to substitute new ribbons next year.

A SHINY coating of crimson "crackle" paint makes the grapevine base of this wreath look good enough to eat, while its glossy red surface complements the bright clusters of artificial fruit. This paint, available at most craft stores, can be sprayed on in colors or added as a clear final coat over other paint. Once painted, the base was embellished by hot gluing greenery, pine cones, fruit, and paper ribbon into place. Lastly a few sprigs of German statice were hot glued on to give the composition a snowy appearance.

GOLD ranks right behind red and green in the triumvirate of traditional Christmas colors. But it is also a favorite autumn tone, making this wreath an appropriate decoration throughout the Thanksgiving/harvest season as well. It was made by first weaving and twisting olive and gold velvet ribbons through the branches of a silk Canadian pine wreath. Next a green bow was hot glued on at the bottom. Finally holiday picks tipped with cones, gold berries, bronze fruit, gold leaves, and ornaments were hot glued into place.

SOME wreaths start with an attractive base. Others begin with an idea. This one was inspired by a rosy cheeked, ceramic Santa Claus face that seems perfectly framed in its halo of ribbon and greenery. Look over your own collection of Christmas treasures—it might inspire a new life for an old decoration. This wreath was made by first attaching a 2-1/4" by 4" (5.7 by 10 cm) block of styrofoam to an 18" (45 cm) vine base with hot glue and wire. Stems of vinyl spruce branches were stuck into the foam with the greenery spread out across the upper right half of the base. The Santa face was wired to the base. Then a bow of red plaid ribbon was secured above his head with streamers weaved through the spruce and hot glued to the base. Artificial berries and apples were hot glued randomly through the greens along with dried globe amaranth, small dried mushrooms, and twigs.

L A R G E, hollow grapevine bases such as this 36" (90 cm) one make for grand decorative statements when adorned with elements that are bold enough to complement their significant size. Nowadays these bases are available at florist or craft shops. Or you can make your own by first forming four or five hoops of vine about 8" (20 cm) diameter and using these as supports to interweave a large circle of vines perpendicular to them. Here the artful use of a few lengths of wide ribbon and silk poinsettia combine to create this lovely Christmas wreath. The ribbon was entwined through the base and hot glued at critical points before wiring on the flowers.

A TRADITIONAL
Christmas evergreen takes on a stunning new look in this wreath packed chock full of burgundy colored holly leaves. To make it, first the bow was attached to a grapevine base with hot glue. Then the holly was glued on in small branch clusters. Lastly the berries, plums, and lipidium were picked and glued into place. (When possible, it's usually best to attach the most fragile component last to prevent damage when adding other materials.)

FRESH cranberries and bowls of mixed nuts are so popular at Christmas time that we immediately associate them with the holiday season. Used in a wreath, they send a cheerful Yuletide greeting that's bright in color and rich in texture. To make this wreath, simply start by hot gluing the nuts evenly around the top, the inner, and the outer edges of a 10" (25 cm) styrofoam base. Fill in the spaces with hot glued cranberries. This wreath took two packages of cranberries and one of mixed nuts. You may want to spray paint the base red first or wrap it with red ribbon so you won't need as many berries to cover the base.

THERE'S no rule that requires you to leave an empty space in the middle of a wreath. Why not use it as an opportunity to frame a treasured keepsake like this ceramic Father Christmas, which lends old-world charm to this lovely Yuletide creation. The designer simply wired old St. Nick into a purchased vinyl blue spruce wreath and hot glued in some cones, dried pomegranates, pepperberries, silk flowers, iridescent clear glass balls, and tiny homemade Christmas packages. She tied a bow in 8 yds. (7.3 m) of ribbon, hot glued it in place and used the excess to loop loosely through the greenery.

GREENS and reds are certainly the most commonly used Christmas colors, but that doesn't mean you must restrict yourself to traditional holly berries and pine boughs to capture their holiday spirit. Here's a stunning wreath ablaze with red roses that would make an ideal Yule adornment or a tasteful year-round decoration. Begin by wrapping a straw base with green velvet ribbon, leaving about 3" (7.5 cm) uncovered at the bottom. Insert the stems of a dozen or so silk roses and a few sprays of artificial greenery into the straw to cover the exposed area. Use pearl-head pins to fasten a ruffle of red velvet ribbon around the front surface and hot glue a silk rose blossom under each loop.

CINNAMON sticks provide an attractive perch in this imaginative table wreath that brings a touch of nature indoors. Use it to brighten any holiday buffet or to display throughout the year on a mantlepiece or side table. Start by hot gluing two cinnamon sticks vertically to a 12" (30 cm) vine base, then tie the third one across the others with wire, raffia, or string before securing with more glue. Cover the joints with hot glued moss. Likewise attach miniature lotus pods, artificial apples, painted cane twigs, mushrooms, evergreens, moss, and finally the birds. Poppy pods could be substituted for the lotus, and pomegranates for the apples. You could also attach a wet foam block and use fresh flowers and greens instead of the dried materials.

I T'S   N O T   always necessary or advisable to cover a particularly attractive wreath base when you can make it part of your design. In this Victorian floral wreath, a cluster of twisted tamboo sets off and complements the sinuous lines of its grapevine base. The tamboo was fastened to the base with wire. Then the large parchment silk flowers, pine branches, berries, more small flowers, and pieces of cup leaf were added with hot glue.

So You want to make just one more wreath. But you have nothing to use for a base. You're out of greenery and flowers. All the ornaments are hung on the tree. And the last of the ribbon was used long ago. There's nothing left but some paint, glitter, and a glue gun. Believe it or not, you have the makings for a wreath!

This probably isn't a wreath you'd want to hang on your front door, but it illustrates a handy technique for making letters, numbers, and all sorts of other shapes to decorate your holiday creations. Simply coat a piece of glass with cooking oil spray and squirt hot glue around and around to form a circle, dropping glitter between each layer. Once it cools the glue lifts off easily and can be painted on the back to add color. This "wreath" took a little over three 10" (25 cm) sticks of hot glue.

No sound is more evocative of Christmas than the clear, angelic tones of a French horn. Here the warmth of those inspiring melodies is captured in a wreath made by temporarily embellishing the instrument as a holiday decoration. Obviously the French horn is not an item one normally has lying around the house (unless you're the parent of a school band student). It is included as a reminder that your imagination can lead you to create wreaths from almost anything, often with marvelous results. This one was made by attaching a circle of red punch ribbon to the horn with gold pipe cleaners. Red foil paper was inserted into the bell along with a block of floral foam. Stalks of red glitter ting-ting (available in florist or craft shops) were inserted into the foam. The musical staff and notes were made from hot glue.

A T N O time of
year are we more aware
of nature's changing
cycles than in autumn, when we
reap what was sown in the spring.
For centuries, in agrarian societies
the world over, woven circles of
freshly cut grain were essential
elements of harvest celebrations.
More than mere decoration, these
early wreaths were sacred talismans,
lovingly wrought in the hopes of
pleasing the gods and assuring
another successful planting.

Today's harvest wreaths borrow
from these traditions, often
incorporating fruits, grains, nuts,
and other fall gatherings in their
designs. The blazing reds and
yellows of autumn leaves offer a
pallet of color unique to the season,
making harvest time a favorite for
wreath makers.

A FEELING of wild natural growth, of seed pods ready to drop, of berries to be gathered for the coming winter—all combine in this striking autumn creation. The designer began by making a vine base interwoven with freshly cut bittersweet and wired together. To this she hot glued groups of preserved oak leaves, dried mushrooms, lambs wool, okra, mahogany pods, plastic berries, globe amaranth, straw flowers, and finally protea, which was wired and glued into place. The bow was wired together and attached at the top with the ribbon threaded back and forth through the foliage and wired to sticks at the ends.

NATURE'S bounty seems to positively burst from this wreath centered around a horn of plenty and accented with colorful leaves and gourds. The designer began with a 14" (35 cm) straw base, which she covered with bunches of yarrow approximately 7-9" (17.5-22.5 cm) long. Each bunch was tied off with a rubber band and wired to the straw, overlapping the previous bunch. The horn of plenty shape can be made from styrofoam, wadded and taped newspaper, or cardboard. This one was then covered with eucalyptus leaves hot glued over the surface in an overlapping pattern. The finished horn was picked and hot glued to the base. Sharpened picks and an occasional dab of hot glue were used to add gourds, garlic cloves, apples, lotus pods, chestnut pods, mahogany pods, oak leaves, and bittersweet.

MUTED browns and golds suggest autumn as an ideal time to make and display this dramatic Victorian wreath, made more interesting and unusual by the use of dried artichokes. These eye-catching design elements are easy to prepare: You can buy them at your local supermarket and hang them by their stems to dry. You may want to spray on a bit of fixative to bring out the natural color and add a matte finish to the artichokes. To make this wreath, start by hot gluing dried caspia and silk fantasia cone flowers to an oval grapevine base and entwine a length of peach lace through the composition. Then wire on the artichokes and a few pine cones.

NATURE saves her most fiery, passionate colors for the fall of the year, so why not bring that natural warmth indoors by decorating your home with a few of those fallen leaves you've been raking from the lawn? This blazing autumn wreath was made on a grapevine base by hot gluing in German statice, preserved oak leaves, cane cones, and clusters of picked yarrow.

ONE of the most important design skills is knowing when to do nothing. The maker of this harvest wreath recognized the simple grace of this swirling grapevine base and added just the right amount of soft colors, shapes, and textures to enhance its form without overpowering its natural beauty. She hot glued sprays of artemisia at the bottom so it flowed outward to echo the lines in the vines. Della robia fruit was hot glued on, adding full rounded forms and warm burgundy tones that were repeated in her choice of paper ribbon for the bow.

A BOUNTY of fruits and scented spices bathed in the warm earth tones of autumn make this a classic harvest wreath. The designer began by pinning colored twist paper onto a purchased straw base so that loops of the paper puffed out at 2" (5 cm) intervals. Onto this background she hot glued plastic fruit that had been rolled first in white glue and then in a mixture of spices: turmeric, oregano, parsley flakes, mustard, chili pepper, cinnamon, cloves, and marjoram. A twist paper bow and small bouquets of baby's breath and cinnamon sticks were hot glued on to complete the composition.

FLOWERS normally make us think of spring and summer, but the use of silk flowers in soft warm tones gives this wreath a decidedly autumnal flavor. It's one you can use throughout the year or put away until the next appropriate season or occasion. It was made on a grapevine base by hot gluing picked clusters of peach lipidium, silk flowers, nuts, cones, and artificial fruits.

A L L the colors, the shapes, and the textures of autumn are tastefully combined with the bounty of a fruitful harvest in this big and bold composition. The designer began by stuffing a large hollow grapevine base with fresh fruit (although you may want to use artificials to reduce the weight). Then he wired a few ears of Indian corn at the top and hot glued pampas grass and pyracantha berries around the base. A few stalks of dried wheat complete the design.

WEDDINGS, anniversaries, and St. Valentine's Day are special occasions when we proclaim our affection and dedication to those we love most. So why not create a very personal message by expressing your love with a homemade wreath?

H E R E ' S a dandy double wedding wreath that does double duty at the reception. The central flower arrangement is actually the bride's bouquet, which traditionally gets tossed (and lost) to an eager guest before everyone has a chance to admire it. By wiring the arrangement temporarily to this clever wreath and hanging it behind the wedding cake, the bouquet provides a lovely backdrop for the cutting ceremony, where the photographer will surely capture it forever in the wedding scrapbook.

The wreath was made out of two 24" (60 cm) straw bases by cutting one, linking it into the other, and wiring the two securely together. The interlocked bases were then wrapped with white satin ribbon. Lace, tulle, strands of pearls, and a miniature veil were pinned to the bride's wreath. Black satin bows were pinned to the groom's side along with a top hat cut from poster board and painted.

ONE could almost imagine a runner of ivy growing naturally to form this lovely Valentine wreath. The secret to its airy design is the hand crafted wire base made from six 18" (45 cm) lengths of 18-gauge wire. Three pieces of wire were bent into shape and taped together for each side of the heart shape, then entwined with silk ivy. Three lengths of different colored thin satin ribbon were tied in love knots every 6" (15 cm) or so, then hot glued into place irregularly around the heart with a bow made from the excess. Dried flowers were hot glued on in the following order: German statice, straw flowers, celosia, roses, and globe amaranth.

Yo u can almost hear the love birds cooing on this frilly white wedding wreath that combines matrimonial symbolism with bridal accessories in a composition for which the occasion is unmistakable. First a heart-shaped straw base was covered with white paper ribbon, then a layer of glitzy opalescent ribbon, and finally wrapped loosely with white lace. Corsage pins were used to fasten a handmade bridal veil to the top and a garter to the side. The doves were hot glued into place. An opalescent ribbon bow and strands of pearls complete the effect.

S ENDING messages of affection expressed through the language of flowers is a tradition that has thrived since the Victorian Age. This dainty heart-shaped wreath delivers its missive with delicate dried materials and potpourri. To make it, first coat the top and sides of a store-bought styrofoam base with craft glue and press green potpourri into the surface. Let the glue dry completely before hot gluing the flowers. This wreath has white daisies for innocence, hibiscus for delicate beauty, mint for virtue, fern for sincerity, pansies to say, "You occupy my thoughts," and red salvia to cover any bare spots.

TH I S lacy heart-shaped wreath would make a thoughtful gift for Valentine's Day or a lovely wedding decoration. Embellished with fresh roses, its beauty will change with the season as the flowers dry in place. It was made on a straw base by first pinning ruffled lace around the heart with hot glued Spanish moss added to cover the pins. The stems of six Madam Delbarde roses were broken off about 1" (2.5 cm) from the bloom and replaced with wire pierced through the stem. The wires were covered with floral tape and poked into the base. A few sprigs of blue eucalyptus and bows of pink ribbon complete the design.

IF Y O U have a wreath in mind but can't find just the right base, don't hesitate to improvise. Our designer cut a bold heart shape from a sheet of balsa wood to create this sassy St. Valentine's Day wreath. Start with any lightweight wood or a sheet of styrofoam and cut out the desired shape with a jig saw. This one was painted with red latex enamel before adding a paper doily, curling ribbon and two more hearts cut out of wood.

The Victorian tradition of floral symbolism inspired this all natural wedding wreath that reads like sacred marriage vows spoken in the language of flowers and herbs. There are roses to signify love, carnations to represent the bonds of affection, globe amaranth and cockscomb for undying love, thyme for strength and courage, rosemary for remembrance and fidelity, sage for domestic virtue, lavender for devotion, and blue salvia to say, "I'm thinking of you." The designer began by bending a heavy coat hanger into a circle and wiring artemesia around it to form a base. More artemesia was tied on with fishing line before hot gluing the dried herbs and flowers into place.

W EDDINGS bring months of preparation, hours of joyful celebration, and a lifetime of treasured memories. A personalized bridal wreath will brighten the occasion and become a cherished keepsake for years to come. This one was made by first laying several yards of rose lace on a table, gathering it around a straw base, and securing with pins to resemble "leg of mutton" sleeves. Each gather was wrapped with pink satin ribbon and a bow. A bouquet of blue silk flowers was pinned to the base along with a garter, a gold necklace, and a pair of antique earrings—something old, something new, something borrowed, and something blue.

A S M A L L heart-shaped greenery wreath purchased at a local craft store was embellished with dried flowers and ribbon to create this very personal Valentine's Day statement. The greenery was filled in with German statice and baby's breath before hot gluing the flowers into place. Included are celosia, globe amaranth, straw flowers, pepperberries and a few roses for love. A lovely pink bow adds just the right finishing touch.

WHAT image could better express the essence of matrimony than two rings, like two lives or spirits, linked and growing together? This dainty double wreath captures the feeling perfectly with red roses for love and pink roses for romance on a natural background suggestive of bridal lace. The base was formed by taping together two rings of heavy galvanized (clothes line) wire and covering it with wired-on clumps of Spanish moss. Silver king artemisia was wired on in bunches starting from the top and working along each ring in one direction from the outside to the inside. Then the roses, straw flowers, baby's breath, hyacinth, dusty miller, and globe amaranth were hot glued around the rings, concentrating them at the top.

F E W can afford to mark each wedding anniversary with a gift of precious metals or gemstones, but a thoughtfully designed wreath can restate the many facets of a lasting relationship through artistic floral composition. In this anniversary design we see love expressed with roses, devotion represented by lavender, remembrance and fidelity proclaimed in rosemary, unfading affection demonstrated though cockscomb and globe amaranth, joy and happiness professed with marjoram, strength and courage noted in thyme, and the bonds of affection celebrated with carnations. The designer first made a base by securing bunches of artemisia to a bent coat hanger using fishing line. The dried flowers and herbs (which also included larkspur and straw flowers) were attached with hot glue along with the wired moiré bow.

R EACHING your fiftieth year of marriage is both an accomplishment and an occasion for celebration. This golden anniversary wreath commemorates the day in grand style with a shiny gilded circle to represent the wedding band and hearts and roses for love. It was made by first covering a purchased straw wreath base with metallic gold wrapping paper secured with hot glue. Two styrofoam hearts were likewise covered, then tied together with red ribbon and hot glued on. The numbers, silk roses, and bows were also attached with hot glue.

As MORE and more people discover the fun and gratification of making Christmas wreaths, they eventually turn their attention and talents toward other holidays throughout the year. Easter, with its rich symbolism and close association with springtime flowers, is a perfect time to commemorate with a wreath. Mother's Day, Father's Day, Halloween, and St. Patrick's Day also offer exciting design possibilities. Once you master the simple techniques of wreath making, you'll want to decorate your home with a wreath for every holiday.

EASTER

FOR the young and the young at heart, the Easter season heralds the coming of a mischievous bunny who conceals colorful candy eggs for children to search out and recover. This lovely table wreath captures the spirit with a soft fuzzy bunny, a basket of Easter treasures, and a little bear to assist. It was made from a purchased greenery wreath to which the three central items were fastened with satin ribbon. Eight silk roses were hardened with petal porcelain solution (available in craft stores) and coated with acrylic paint along with eight wooden eggs. Once dry these were fastened to the base with hot glue. A few silk leaves were hot glued to the roses for contrast and texture.

S O F T colors, lacy ribbon, and a stuffed rabbit "depression doll" give an antique country flavor to this tasteful Easter wreath. The maker began with a purchased grapevine form, wrapped it loosely with antique lace ribbon, and covered the ends with a large bow. She attached parchment grape leaves by entwining the stems into the base, then added silk flowers and berries with hot glue. Finally the rabbit was secured to the base with wire.

74

T H E religious symbolism of the Easter holiday is captured in this reverent tribute to resurrection and renewal. The designer chose a vine base not unlike a crown of thorns. She fashioned a cross from dried equisetum (also known as horsetail fern or snakegrass), secured it with floral tape, and hot glued it into place. Rattail celosia was added in rays emanating from the base of the cross, where she hot glued a grouping of globe amaranth and button mums. A trinity of yellow sweetheart roses was added to suggest rising from beneath the cross.

THE earliest wreaths probably originated as headwear that later found a home on a wall or door. Here's a lovely Easter bonnet wreath that likewise serves both purposes. It was made on a purchased straw hat to which silk flowers and pink and blue netting were first hot glued around the center. More netting was used to make a large bow. Finally ribbon was entwined through the flowers and several multi-colored strands left to dangle from the back of the hat.

JELLYBEAN colors, bunnies, and decorative eggs are harbingers of Easter, especially for young children. Here's a simple wreath that captures the holiday spirit with a cuddly gift that will be appreciated long after the candy is gone. It was made by first wrapping a styrofoam base with purple satin ribbon. Then the toy rabbit was hot glued into place with a papier mache egg glued to its paws. German statice, canella berries, and a few artificial berries were glued in around the bunny with a touch of Easter grass added for sparkle. A bow of lacy pink tulle completes the picture.

ST. PATRICK'S DAY

HERE'S a simple, festive, holiday wreath that will keep you in clover on St. Patrick's Day. Start by wrapping a straw or foam wreath base with bright yellow ribbon. Make the shamrocks by forming two loops and one "stem" of green ribbon into the shape of a clover and secure these to the base with pearl pins.

'**T**w **A** **s** the verdant hills of the Emerald Isle, the leprechaun, and his pots of gold that inspired this lush green tribute to the patron saint of Ireland. To create this floral masterpiece first squeeze a 14" (35 cm) straw base into an oval shape. Next make 1" (2.5 cm) long "hair pins" out of 18 gauge wire and use these to secure about a hundred galax leaves (stems removed) in an overlapping pattern around the entire base. Wire a small round wet-foam floral block to the lower left side of the base and insert Oregon fern, seracena lilies (swamp lily or pitcher plant), Connecticut king lilies (or other yellow flowers), and fresh baby blue eucalyptus into the foam. Secure the pots of gold candy coins to the base and foam with large wire hair pins.

DESIGNER'S TIP

Want your natural greenery to last longer? Before making her wreaths or arrangements, floral designer Janet Frye treats her ferns and leaves with a mixture of four parts water and one part acrylic floor wax. For large amounts of greenery you can mix it up in a bucket and dunk the greens to coat the entire surface. Just shake off the excess and let the leaves dry before using. Use the same mixture in a spray mister to apply to a finished arrangement.

A **B A T** silhouetted against the harvest moon...leaves rustling in the autumn wind... a jack-o'-lantern flickering in the cool darkness... With all that Halloween imagery, it's no wonder our wreath designer added garlic cloves to ward off the vampires! To make this spooky hoop she first wrapped a 12" (30 cm) styrofoam base with 3 yds. (270 cm) of #40 black satin ribbon. She covered a 5" (12.5 cm) foam circle with 10 yds. (9 m) of #3 yellow ribbon, added a bat cut out of black velvet, and hot glued the circle to the ring. A chunk was cut out of the plastic pumpkin to make it fit nicely on the ring. Finally the flat leaf eucalyptus leaves and garlic cloves were hot glued into place.

A **H O M E M A D E** ghost and spider highlight this Halloween wreath. It was created by first spray painting a grapevine base black and adding gold glitter. The ghost was made from a rectangle of white cloth wrapped around polyfill and tied with an orange ribbon. Eyes were added with a marking pen. The spider was done in a similar manner from a circle of black material snipped on the skirt to form legs. A bow made from Halloween ribbon was wired to the top and white ghost branches were hot glued on. The ghost was wired to the base, while the spider dangles mysteriously from nearly invisible webbing purchased at a craft store.

80

HALLOWEEN

IT'S easy to turn everyday store-bought decorations into a one-of-a-kind holiday wreath as this designer did with elements found at a local craft shop. Once you establish a focal point for your design—in this case the pre-made spider and web—all you need are a few complementary accessories. This one uses a purchased twig wreath base on which the web was pinned and hot glued into place along with a novelty ghost and plastic cauldron. To balance the look she hot glued on an arrangement of dried German statice, nigella pods, and a few artificial apples.

MOTHER'S DAY

BURSTING with red and pink floral splendor, this creation seems an obvious choice for remembering your favorite loved one on Mother's Day. In addition, the use of silk and preserved flowers makes it a remarkably durable keepsake that can be enjoyed for some time to come. Start with a grapevine base and hot glue the silk flowers, then the ivy into place. Pick and glue the dried roses, globe amaranth, and caspia in clusters and fill in any bare spots with moss.

HERE'S an elegant Mother's Day greeting delivered though the language of flowers. In Victorian times the rose was used as an expression of love, the color white signified purity, and the circle represented undying affection. So this wreath delivers a message any mother would enjoy. It was made on a straw base to which sixteen pink silk roses and their leaves were attached with hot glue. Six yards (5.5 m) of 3" (7.5 cm) satin ribbon was formed into a bow that was pinned to the base at the top, while the ends were wound through the leaves and tied into a smaller bow at the bottom. Then two small pink silk rose buds were hot glued to the bow. Sprigs of baby's breath were hot glued in to add contrast.

TREASURED mementos can add special significance to your holiday creations as in this very personal Mother's Day wreath. It was made on a straw base covered first with white paper ribbon, then wrapped again with glitzy iridescent ribbon and pink tulle. Then the hat, gloves, pearls, family photos, and a tussy mussy were wired or hot glued into place.

THIS nostalgic, country-flavored Mother's Day wreath would surely evoke a smile from a mom who has fond memories of homemade butter and family evenings gathered around the radio. It was made by first weaving parchment grapevine leaves and the stems of silk flowers into an oval grapevine base. Next a bow of lace-trimmed polka dot ribbon was wired into the arrangement. A 7" (17.5 cm) piece of the ribbon was folded into a fan and wired on along with another small bow. The butter churn and radio were hot glued to their ribbon backgrounds.

S P R I N G colors, ribbons, and pearls light up this Mother's Day remembrance. It was made on a vine base into which freshly-cut purple hyacinth bean was woven. Mexican sage was hot glued to the base beginning at the top and working down each side. Then straw flowers, globe amaranth, zinnias, and bee balm were added to fill out the design. Bells of Ireland were likewise fastened at even intervals with pearls glued into the center of each. Two colors of 1/4" (6.25 mm) ribbon were glued to the top and wrapped down the left side with another pair added on the right.

A SELECTION of fragrant feminine gifts are featured in this thoughtful Mother's Day wreath. The items can be removed from their decorative boxes, leaving the wreath intact for display in mother's bathroom or boudoir. Start with a purchase artificial greenery wreath and tie the gift boxes and a potpourri on with peach colored cord, bending the wire branches around the cord to anchor them in place. Entwine a length of white lace randomly through the greenery and hot glue on several pink silk roses.

FATHER'S DAY

GAME bird feathers and a pair of well-used pipes distinguish this masculine Father's Day wreath as a handsome year-round decoration for any wood-paneled office or sportsman's den. The designer started with an oval grapevine base and wired on eucalyptus sprays in a radiating background pattern to which she hot glued sprays of German statice, gold wind branches, and berry picks. Three silk magnolias were wired on as focal points of the composition with guinea and duck feathers glued in to vary the texture and augment the woodsy theme. Lastly the pipes and bird nest were hot glued to the base.

HERE'S a different approach to wreath shaping that's sure to score a hole-in-one with any golfing dad on Father's Day. It's a striking, yet simple design that could be modified for any occasion (or favorite activity) through the use of different natural materials and accessories. To make the frame/base, cut a piece of cardboard to the desired shape. This one is 12" by 24" (30 by 60 cm). Glue a piece of burlap or other fabric to the cardboard and hot glue bamboo (available at garden supply stores) or any other straight sticks around the edge. Using wire and hot glue, attach a wet foam floral block to the frame and insert horsetail ferns, yellow sweetheart roses (the flower for June), pittosporum, mushrooms, moss, and bear grass into the block. Hot glue wire or a wood pick to the bottom of the plastic figure (this one is a cake decoration) and stick it into the wet foam.

H E R E ' S a unique, versatile, masculine wreath that would look great hanging on the wall or standing on a trophy shelf or mantelpiece. The designer used the handle from a funeral basket (available at flower shops) as the wreath ring by wiring and hot gluing a piece of styrofoam to the bottom. He then covered the foam with sheet moss and paper tree bark and pinned the deer on as a focal point. Mixed scraps of silk greenery, cattails, and gold glitter branches were picked into the foam.

YoU don't need to wait
for a holiday to make a
wreath. Why not give a
wreath as a birthday gift? Or design
one to congratulate a loved one for
an award or personal achievement?
You can make a wreath to liven up
your next party. Or as a centerpiece
to decorate a buffet table. Once you
find out how easy and fun they are
to make, any excuse is a good
excuse for making a wreath.

A D V E N T

T H E four Sundays before Christmas mark the season of Advent, a time of joyous preparation. What better way to get ready for the coming holiday than to set your table around an Advent wreath displaying a candle for each week of the season. Our designer began by wrapping artificial greenery around and through a wire base. Then hot glue was used to secure baby's breath, silk flowers, grape picks, and small bouquets of Russian sage and salvia. A length of ribbon was draped around the surface and a circular brass candle holder nestled in the center. (Just be sure not to leave the lit candles untended and to change them as they melt down.)

R E T I R E M E N T

IF W E think of a holiday as any time spent away from our job, then retirement must be the greatest holiday of all! So why not commemorate the occasion for a loved one with a reminder of those carefree days to come? With these thoughts in mind, the designer of this wreath included the requisite gold watch, a pair of straw hats for puttering around the garden, sunglasses for days at the beach, a park bench

for feeding the birds, a picnic basket for hikes in the mountains, a book for rainy days, a net hammock for napping, and even a mirrored pond with a dangling fishing line for all those lazy hours in between. It's an easy wreath to make once the props are assembled. She started with a grapevine base, hot glued on some mountain moss and artificial greenery, then glued the other items to the base and hung the watch by its chain.

PROMOTION

FE W holidays or occasions bring more lasting
good cheer than a job promotion. We all yearn
for these all too infrequent opportunities: to get
out of the rat race, to climb the ladder of success, to
pluck riches from the trees. This designer called on
these universal themes to commemorate a friend's new-
found good fortune with this humorous gift wreath. She
cut the oval "racetrack" out of foam core, spray painted
it black, and used a silver paint marker to add the lane
stripes and edging. Then the plastic rats were hot glued
to the track. Next she glued a 3" (7.5 cm) square piece
of styrofoam to the lower back side of the track. She
inserted larkspur and rat-tail celosia (pun intended) into
the foam along with money flowers made of folded bills
attached to wire stems with floral tape. (Any currency or
denomination will do.) The purchased wooden ladder
was attached to the foam with wire and glue.

PARTIES

HERE'S an inexpensive, easy-to-make wreath that's literally bursting with color. It's just the thing for a child's birthday party (provided you have someone with lots of "hot air" and strong fingers—this one took fifty-five balloons of assorted colors). Start by making a 21" (52.5 cm) diameter base out of wire and tape. Inflate the balloons to about 5" (12.5 cm) and tie them tightly. (Under-inflating the balloons keeps them more pliable and less likely to pop.) Tie the ends of the balloons to the wire base. Weave ribbons in assorted colors around and between the balloons and tie the excess into a multi-colored bow. Party favors, horns, and other novelties suitable to the occasion could be tied on with more ribbon. You may want to spray the balloons with a four-to-one mixture of water and acrylic floor wax (before adding ribbon) to keep them shiny.

COLORFUL streaming ribbons dancing on air make a grand statement in this dramatic yet easy-to-make party wreath. Ideal for a bridal or baby shower, it could also brighten up a birthday party or sway in the breeze at a backyard cookout. To make it, just cover a straw base with the appropriate color of #40 ribbon and cut as many 6" (180 cm) or longer pieces of #3 ribbon as you need. (This one took thirty-two.) Wrap each streamer once around the base and secure it with two pearl pins, leaving a short length above and a long length below the base. Gather the upper streamers and tie a knot for a hanger, then curl the lower streamers. You may need to re-adjust a few pins to make it hang evenly.

H ERE'S a quick and easy table wreath to highlight a luncheon buffet, an hors d'oeuvre spread for a baby shower, a child's party, or even an Easter gathering. Shown here with a candle, this wreath could also encircle a bowl of snacks, dip, or mints. All you need is a styrofoam base, some gumdrops, and a box of toothpicks. Just break the picks in half, insert the thick end of each into a gumdrop and cover the base. (Just don't expect this one to last long if you have any sweet-tooth friends around.)

T HE defining feature of a wreath is its unbroken border, a symbol of continuity and the cycles of nature. While most wreaths are circular, they may also be elliptical, squared, rectangular, or in the case of this child's birthday party wreath, a pentagon formed around a star. It was made by first spray painting a purchased styrofoam star, then covering each point with a party hat. Different colored curly ribbons were hot glued to the top of each hat and tied together to create the border. Six paper party plates were fastened by cutting a hole in the center of each and hot gluing birthday candles through the plates and into the base. More ribbon and tufts of colored netting were added as a finishing touch.

GET WELL

THE only thing vaguely entertaining about wearing a plaster cast is collecting signatures from visiting well-wishers. Here's a get-well-soon wreath that's sure to cheer up an injured loved one and provide a better (and less aromatic) keepsake than the real thing. Start with a 10" (25 cm) wire wreath form and wrap it with two rolls of gauze. (You might want to pad the base first to give a fuller, more rounded look.) Coat the gauze with thin plaster, joint compound, or wallpaper paste, and let it harden overnight into a round "cast." Hot glue eight dried yellow roses in a crescent shape at the bottom. To make the large flower, insert loops of wire into four uninflated balloons and shape the wire into petals. Use a different colored fifth balloon without wire in the center. Use floral tape to hold the flower together and hot glue it to the base in the center of the roses. Make a bow out of thin curling ribbon and hot glue it to the base. Let friends sign the "cast" before presenting it and leave a marking pen so later visitors can add their names.

VACATION

DEPENDING on where you live, the word "holiday" might suggest a commemoration or a vacation. But no matter where you are, a little time away from work is something to be celebrated, so why not try making a vacation wreath? Add elements that suggest your destination: tulips, wooden shoes, and a windmill for a trip to Holland; heather, roses, and a castle turret for a getaway to Britain; sea shells, sunglasses, and tanning lotion for a week at the beach. You could even build the family's excitement before the trip by including airplane tickets and a countdown calendar showing the days remaining before departure.

Our designer chose a tropical theme for this vacation wreath. She first cut a styrofoam base in the shape of a tropical island hut and covered it with melaleuca bark using rubber cement. She picked in dried long-leaf eucalyptus, silk hibiscus, and dendrobium orchids for color and completed the vacation motif with a souvenir lei and a toy camera.

99

NEW BABY

No EVENT could be more deserving of commemoration than the arrival of a new baby. Both mother and child will appreciate this wreath as a gift that keeps on giving. A styrofoam base was first wrapped with satin ribbon, then wrapped again with white tulle. Lengths of colorful curling ribbon were used to tie the baby toys directly to the base, with hot glue added in a few places to secure the items. A bow of red tulle ribbon and more curling ribbon were added for color.

A N Y newborn would be comforted to see the cheerful dancing bear smiling down from its perch in this thoughtful baby shower wreath, a gift that will please the expected child as well as the expectant mother. To make it, the bear was first tied into a purchased artificial greenery wreath with peach and red satin ribbon with several bows and streamers added on the neck and side. Two yards (183 cm) of 1-1/2" (3.75 cm) white lace were entwined in the branches and hot glued in place along with several red silk rose buds and more pink satin bows.

SO F T and wooly dried pampas grass gives this wreath the feel of a cuddly warm blanket, making it an ideal gift to celebrate a new addition to the family. And long afterwards, the stuffed animal will remind the parents (and someday the child) of your thoughtfulness. The pampas grass was woven into a grapevine base, then the toy and the bow were wired in place. Hot glue was used to attach zinnia, swamp sunflower, German statice, and delphinium.

WHETHER it's a boy or a girl, any newborn would adore the happy clown and grinning crescent moon on this cheerful nursery wreath. Make one for your own child or as a thoughtful, personal gift for a friend's baby shower. And not just for the mother: the clown will become a hugable companion for the growing infant. Start by randomly spray painting highlights of yellow, blue, and pink on an oval grapevine base. Cut the smiling moon out of cardboard and first paint it silver (as a reflective base coat) before applying three coats of yellow. Once it's dry you can add the face with folk art paint. Hot glue a few pipe cleaners to the cardboard and tie it onto the base. Use multi-colored curly ribbon to attach the clown.

CHILD'S ACCOMPLISHMENT

AFTER Christmas and birthdays, the first day of school is probably the most anticipated event of early childhood. Here's a wreath that not only commemorates the coming milestone, but also provides a place (other than the refrigerator) to pin papers and drawings brought home from class. It was made by first covering a purchased straw base with pages of folded notebook paper secured with pins. The pompon (displaying the school color) was attached with a florist pin, while the pencils and ruler were tied on with ribbon. A package of gold stick-on stars pinned to the base allows the parent to add special awards for exceptional papers.

MARDI GRAS

M A R D I G R A S or Shrove
Tuesday, the last day before Lent, is celebrated around the world with carnivals,
masquerade balls, and parades of marching costumed
merrymakers. It's a great excuse for a party and a perfect
occasion for a sparkling festive wreath. This one was
made by first spray painting a straw base gold and wrapping it with gold and purple ribbons. A purple bow on a
gold punch ribbon background was pinned to the base
with more gold and green curly ribbon dangling from it.
The plastic masks were hot glued into place and multi-
colored ornaments wired on.

104

ERE'S a quick and easy wreath that will bring the carnival atmosphere of Mardi Gras to your next party. All you need is a straw wreath base, a bag of shredded gold foil (available at craft stores), a colorful bow, and a party mask. Lay the foil out so you can pick up the strands in bunches and loop them inside a U-shaped florist pin. Stick the loaded pins into the base until it is completely covered. Attach the bow, mask, and a few streamers of ribbon with more florist pins.

NEW YEAR'S EVE

NOISEMAKERS, shooting stars, and silvery ribbons invite revelry in a wreath that would enliven any party, especially a New Year's Eve bash or a masquerade ball. Start by covering a straw base with a double layer of white satin rib- bon and wrap it again with gold foil punch ribbon. Make a bow of gold and silver punch ribbon and wire it to the base. Finally hot glue the horns, wired silver stars (avail- able at craft stores), and clear glass ornaments into place.

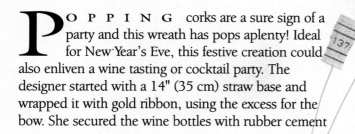

POPPING corks are a sure sign of a party and this wreath has pops aplenty! Ideal for New Year's Eve, this festive creation could also enliven a wine tasting or cocktail party. The designer started with a 14" (35 cm) straw base and wrapped it with gold ribbon, using the excess for the bow. She secured the wine bottles with rubber cement and wooden picks, then hot glued on a pair of plastic champagne glasses. In each glass she placed a party noisemaker, allowing the foil ends to spray out in a burst of color. Wine corks were impaled on spray-painted wires inserted into the base. Fake pink roses were hot glued on, adding softness and texture to the design.

WELCOME

YELLOW ribbons have become synonymous with long awaited homecomings. This "welcome back" wreath, with its yellow ribbon and yellow silk flowers, would brighten up the return of any prodigal son or daughter you might be longing to see. It was made on a grapevine base with the large bows wired into place first. Then the silk greenery and flowers were hot glued on and the small yellow bows added last.

NOTHING is more disorienting than moving into a new home. This lovely gift wreath would surely make life among the boxes more tolerable and remind your new neighbors that they are welcome. It was made by first wiring a bow of tapestry ribbon to a grapevine base, with additional streamers of ribbon cut, knotted, and wired around the edges. Next several sprays of dark green eucalyptus were hot glued in along with picked silk roses, artificial berries, caspia, and pepperberries.

T H E perfect gift to welcome a newcomer to the neighborhood, this cheery wreath would be a much appreciated way to decorate a new neighbor's door, offering a pleasant invitation to other visitors. To make it, parchment grape leaves and silk flowers were woven into a purchased grapevine base. Then a lacy ribbon bow was wired on. The little cloth rabbit and basket were hot glued to the miniature bench, which was likewise fastened to the wreath base.

GRADUATION

WHETHER it be from college, high school, kindergarten, or just a do-it-yourself wallpapering class, graduation days mark significant milestones in our lives. Why should diplomas and tassels be our only keepsakes of these special moments of achievement? Here's a clever mortarboard wreath that not only captures the holiday spirit of graduation day but also adds to your repertoire of potential wreath shapes and components. To make the graduation cap, the designer first cut out a 12" (30 cm) square of foam core, spray painted it glossy black, and glued on some gold ribbon trim. A black plastic bowl was hot glued to the board to complete the cap. A "diploma" of rolled paper tied with black ribbon was hot glued to the surface along with yellow pansies and more gold ribbon for color.

CONTRIBUTING DESIGNERS

NORA BLOSE AND MICHELLE WEST

Nora is an herbalist from Candler, N.C., with a design studio called Nora's Follies. (Pages 54, 92, and 97 top). Michelle is a floral designer for homes, offices, and weddings with an in-home boutique in Asheville, N.C. (Pages 61, 85 bottom, and 109.) They often work together on wreaths and other projects. (Pages 21, 22, 30, 74, 80 bottom, 85 top, 88, and 94.)

JULIANNE BRONDER

is the corporate designer for Van's Floral Products, a wholesale company in Alsip, Ill. Her experience in floral design includes teaching, consulting, and design show presentations. She studied at the American Floral Art School in Chicago, Ill. (Pages 18, 23, 24, 39, 45, 52, 56, 82, and 108 top.)

JANET FRYE

owns The Enchanted Florist shop in Arden, North Carolina. Trained at Adam Eden Florist in Palm Springs, California, Janet has been a floral designer for fifteen years and has taught floral design for seven years. (Pages 28 bottom, 37, 41, 44, 50, 60, 75, 79, 80 top, 90, 95, 96 top, 98, 99, 107, and 110.)

AUBREY GIBSON, ALECIA GODFREY, AND BETH WELCH

are floral designers for Sweet Bouquets Flowers and Gifts in Arden, North Carolina where they often conduct classes in wreath making. (Pages 26, 28 top, 34, 35, 36, 38, 42, 46, 47, 51, 57, 58, 63 top and bottom, 76, 78, 91, 96 bottom, 97 bottom, 103 top, 104, and 106.)

CYNTHIA GILLOOLY

enjoys creating innovative arrangements with both natural and artificial materials. She owns and operates The Golden Cricket florist shop in Asheville, North Carolina. (Pages 27, 29, 32, 77, 81, 100, and 108 bottom.)

JEANNETTE HAFNER

grows the flowers and greenery for her designs in her gardens in Orange, Connecticut. She teaches drying and arranging techniques as well as design classes. (Pages 20, 31, 53, 64, 67, and 70.)

NICOLE VICTORIA

is a free lance designer of Victorian interiors and accessories with a studio in Asheville, North Carolina. She also produces a national wholesale line called the "French Victorian Romance Collection." (Pages 66, 71, 72, 84, 87, 101, 103 bottom, and 105.)

DIANE WEAVER

worked as an art director/designer in Detroit and New York. She and her husband Dick operate Gourmet Gardens herb nursery in Weaverville, North Carolina. She uses some of the 180 herb varieties they grow to design and make wreaths, arrangements, culinary herb mixtures and herb butters. (Pages 48, 68, 86, and 102.)

Also thanks to ...

DAWN CUSICK

(Pages 40 and 62.)

I N D E X

B I B L I O G R A P H Y

Cusick, Dawn. *A Scented Christmas.*
New York: Sterling Publishing
Company, 1990.

Lloyd, Elizabeth Jane. *Enchanted Circles.*
London: Conran Octopus
Limited, 1990.

Pulleyn, Rob. *The Wreath Book.*
New York: Sterling Publishing
Company, 1988.

Taylor, Carol. *Christmas Naturals.*
New York: Sterling Publishing
Company, 1988.